Watery Graves

Carole Wilkinson

sundance

Published by Sundance Publishing
P.O. Box 1326, 234 Taylor Street, Littleton, MA 01460

Copyright © text Carole Wilkinson

First published 1999 as Phenomena by
Horwitz Martin
A Division of Horwitz Publications Pty Ltd
55 Chandos St., St. Leonards NSW 2065 Australia

Exclusive United States Distribution: Sundance Publishing

ISBN 0-7608-4952-8

Printed in Canada

Contents

Author's Note

While researching this book I learned about people and the different ways they react to extreme situations. Whenever I could, I tried to read the accounts written by actual people who experienced a shipwreck. I didn't want someone else's idea of what it might have been like.

One of my most exciting moments was the discovery of a copy of William Strachey's 375-year-old account of the wreck of the *Sea Venture*. It was in a library near where I live. The account had been printed in 1625, only sixteen years after the actual shipwreck. This account really made me feel what it would be like to be on a ship that was about to sink.

Once upon a time Carole Wilkinson was a laboratory technician. She decided that wasn't much fun and now writes books for children and teenagers instead.

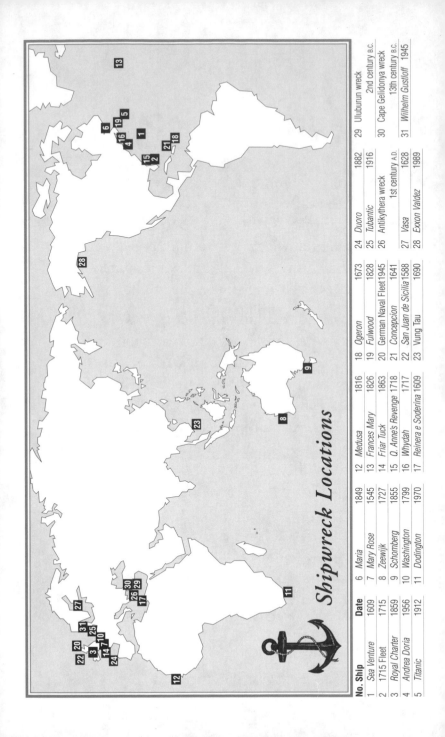

Shipwreck Locations

No.	Ship	Date
1	Sea Venture	1609
2	1715 Fleet	1715
3	Royal Charter	1859
4	Andrea Doria	1956
5	Titanic	1912
6	Maria	1849
7	Mary Rose	1545
8	Zeewijk	1727
9	Schomberg	1855
10	Washington	1799
11	Dodington	1970
12	Medusa	1816
13	Frances Mary	1826
14	Friar Tuck	1863
15	Q. Anne's Revenge	1718
16	Whydah	1717
17	Reinera e Soderina	1609
18	Ogeron	1673
19	Fulwood	1828
20	German Naval Fleet	1945
21	Concepcion	1641
22	San Juan de Sicilia	1588
23	Vung Tau	1690
24	Duoro	1882
25	Tubantic	1916
26	Antikythera wreck	1st century A.D.
27	Vasa	1628
28	Exxon Valdez	1989
29	Uluburun wreck	2nd century B.C.
30	Cape Gelidonya wreck	13th century B.C.
31	Wilhelm Gustloff	1945

Introduction

No one knows exactly how many ships lie in watery graves on the bottom of the ocean. We can only guess. People have been building and sailing boats and ships for at least 11,000 years. Shipwreck experts estimate that one tenth of all of the ships built have been wrecked. That means there must be millions of wrecked ships lying on the seabed.

When a ship is wrecked it is a tragedy. The ship is damaged or destroyed. People often die. Goods are lost. Yet people are fascinated by shipwreck stories—tales of terrible storms, know-it-all captains, and sunken treasure. Part of the fascination of shipwreck stories is finding out how people act when faced with a watery grave.

Sometimes the best sailor in the world can't save a ship in a storm. At other times ships are wrecked in perfect weather because of bad sailors. Often, survival at sea can have more to do

with good luck than good sailing. The best sailors can end up on the bottom of the ocean when their luck turns bad. Yet good luck saves poor sailors in the worst situations.

The misfortune of unlucky sailors can be good luck for people who find the sunken ship. Treasure hunters might find gold coins. Marine archaeologists might find a clue to the past—an ancient oil jar or a 16th century sailor's shoe.

Each shipwreck has its own story. Sometimes it's the ship itself that is interesting. Sometimes it's the way a ship sank that makes it special. Some wrecks are interesting because of the way they were discovered. Every shipwreck has secrets to reveal about human nature.

For thousands of years, ships have been sailing and sinking—taking passengers and crew with them. Yet, people keep going out to sea. Perhaps they think it won't be them. Do *you* feel lucky today?

Chapter 1: Introduction

Imagine . . .

you are Amy Taylor sailing on the Sea Venture to the new colony of Virginia in 1609.

AMY WASN'T SUPPOSED to go on deck by herself. But the ship was rocking so much it made her feel sick to be down below. Her mother was asleep. Surely she wouldn't mind if Amy went up on deck to find her father.

They had been at sea for nearly two months. Amy was tired of being on the *Sea Venture*. She missed their little cottage in England and the green countryside that surrounded it. She missed her own bed with the pink bedspread. She missed the special cakes her mother made. She missed her darling cat, Tom. She couldn't wait until they reached Virginia. She didn't know what to expect there. Did they have cats in Virginia? Whatever was in store for them, Amy was looking forward to setting foot on solid ground again.

A strong wind blew her hair into her eyes as she reached the deck. The powerful wind pushed her back as she walked. She had to hold onto the rail to make sure that a gust of wind didn't carry her away.

Amy searched the deck for her father. The *Sea Venture* wasn't a big ship. It didn't take long for Amy to find him, standing on the bow with the Admiral, Sir George Somers.

Amy was afraid of Sir George. Her father had assured her that he was friendly enough when you got to know him. To Amy he seemed like a gruff old man who didn't like children. She decided to hide in a coil of rope until Sir George left and her father was by himself. The wind brought a fragment of their conversation to her.

"I have never before seen such dark and menacing clouds," Amy heard her father say.

"And the wind," said Sir George. "Have you ever heard such a sound?" The wind through the rigging sounded like wild animals, shrieking and wailing.

The two men started to move away together. Amy called out to her father, but the awful wind blew her words away. He kept on walking. The thick black clouds were now all around the ship. It seemed more like night than day. Rain started to pour down.

The ship was pitching back and forth. Waves were washing over the bow. Amy was too scared to move. She clung onto the ropes with both hands and prayed for the storm to pass quickly.

It didn't pass quickly, though. The storm just kept getting stronger and stronger. The rain became so heavy it seemed to Amy that a river of water was pouring from the sky. Amy was drenched. Sailors were climbing

among the rigging, reefing the sails to slow the *Sea Venture*.

It seemed to make little difference. The wind still drove the ship on. The ship crashed into each wave with such force that Amy thought it would be broken to pieces. One moment the little ship was raised high on an enormous mountain of water. Then it was sliding down, so far down, Amy was sure they must be at the bottom of the ocean.

She lost her grip on the ropes as a huge wave crashed over the bow. Amy thought that she would surely be washed overboard, but a hand reached out of the dark and grabbed hold of her.

"This is no place for a child," the sailor shouted. He gathered her up and almost threw her down the nearest hatchway.

Below decks was a different sort of hell. The stench of vomit made her feel sick. The moans and cries of the passengers were awful to hear. Her mother grabbed Amy, who was now shivering from cold and fear, and wrapped her in a blanket.

"I thought you were lost, my darling," she cried. "I wish we had never left England!"

The storm went on and on. The hatches were nailed shut to stop the water from filling up the ship. Through the portholes there was nothing to see but inky black water and even blacker clouds.

Amy lost track of time. The sky was so dark it was impossible to tell when day ended and night began. Amy thought that they would never see daylight again. She didn't wish for the comforts of home anymore. All she wanted was for the sea to stop heaving, the ship to be still and to see blue sky again. . . .

Chapter 1
Lost at Sea

THE GIANT WAVES and strong winds in the story really happened. In fact, the terrible storm lasted for two whole days. When it was over, people believed that the *Sea Venture* and all those on board had been lost at sea forever.

Lost Where?

The storm had beaten the *Sea Venture*. The ship was leaking so badly, the captain knew it was about to sink. He desperately scanned the horizon. To his relief he saw a speck of land.

The captain sailed the sinking ship straight toward the island. He rammed the *Sea Venture* onto shore as the sea was about to swallow it.

Somehow no one was hurt and everyone cheered the captain. But the captain's smile soon faded when he realized that they were wrecked on Devil's Island. This small piece of land was feared and avoided by all sailors.

Devil's Island?

The survivors soon realized that there were neither devils nor people living on the island. To their surprise, they discovered that it was a paradise. Today this island is called Bermuda.

There was plenty of fruit, wild pigs, birds, and seafood to live on, as well as cedar forests to build with. The *Sea Venture* survivors lived very comfortably on the island for 42 weeks. During that time, they built two new cedar boats.

Ten months after they were thought to be lost at sea, the *Sea Venture* survivors arrived in Virginia. The survivors were in much better shape than the colonists in Virginia. The colonists had little food,

survivors: People who live through a terrible event.

paradise: A beautiful, almost-perfect place.

were suffering from disease, and lived in fear of Indian attacks.

Fact Meets Fiction

The real *Sea Venture* was one of nine ships that were taking settlers to Jamestown in the Virginia colony. Sir George Somers was the admiral of the fleet. John Rolfe, who later married Pocahontas, was also on board.

But Amy is just a character. Her part of the story is not real. We don't know much about the the children on *Sea Venture*. We can only imagine how terrified they must have been.

Terrifying or Inspiring?

The wreck of the *Sea Venture* was surely terrifying. But the story of the stormy shipwreck is exciting and inspiring. At the time of the wreck, the *Sea Venture* story became quite famous.

Many of the survivors wrote best-selling stories about the wreck. Amy's story is based on a true report written by William Strachey. (He was secretary to the governor of the Virginia colony.)

Some people think Mr. Strachey's *Sea Venture* story inspired William Shakespeare to write his last play, *The Tempest. The Tempest* is a fantasy about an island shipwreck. The play was performed in London within two years of the famous shipwreck.

People today are still fascinated by the crushing power of the wind and the ocean. Just look at the many books and films about the sinking of the *Titanic*—the "unsinkable ship" that sank on its maiden voyage. Whether it is a luxury ship, a wooden treasure ship, or a fishing boat, every shipwreck has a story to tell.

The Days of Wood and Sail

In the past, sailing ships like the *Sea Venture* were often quite small. They were made of wood. They depended on the wind filling their sails to move across the ocean.

In those days, once a ship left shore, there was no way to communicate with the rest of the world. Sailors had to rely on their own skills to forecast the weather and predict storms. They had sea charts to tell them where dangerous rocks and reefs were. Unfortunately, the charts weren't always accurate. Traveling by sea in the days of wood and sail was a dangerous business.

maiden voyage: First trip.

The Wind: Sailors' Friend or Foe?

Without wind, a sailing ship couldn't go anywhere. A good strong breeze was what sailors wanted. If the wind began to blow too strongly, it had the power to rip sails to shreds. A raging wind could break masts and even capsize ships. Sometimes a storm became a hurricane, the worst sort of storm. During a hurricane, a sailors' friend, the wind, became a deadly enemy.

What Are Hurricanes?

The storm that almost sank the *Sea Venture* was a hurricane. Hurricanes are huge storms that form in tropical oceans, where the air is humid and the water is warm. As the air is warmed by the water, the warm air rises and meets higher cooler air.

The strong winds of a hurricane are caused by air rushing to replace the warm air that's rising. The result is a ferocious wind blowing in a circular motion. Hurricane winds can blow more than 180 mph and can easily destroy ships.

capsize: To overturn a boat accidentally.

Where Are the Worst Winds?

The warm waters of the Gulf of Mexico are a breeding ground for hurricanes. This is a dangerous part of the world for sailing ships. Spanish sailors in the 16th and 17th centuries discovered the dangers of the Gulf as they headed home from the Americas.

Early in the 16th century, the Spanish had conquered much of South and Central America. They mined huge quantities of gold, silver, and jewels in this New World. They shipped this treasure home to Spain by way of the Gulf of Mexico and the Atlantic Ocean.

Once a year, a fleet of large Spanish ships called galleons left the Americas. They were loaded with treasure meant for the King of Spain. Sailing in fleets guarded by armed ships protected their treasure from pirates and the warships of rival nations. Unfortunately, there was no protection from storms. If a hurricane struck, the loss of treasure could be huge.

To avoid the hurricane season, the fleet had to set sail before June. But there were often delays. Sometimes the fleet didn't leave until July or August—the very worst time for hurricanes.

conquered: Took over by using force; won.

19

During the 200 years of Spanish rule in the Americas, Spain lost hundreds of ships and tons of treasure to hurricanes.

Shipwrecks full of sunken treasure capture the imagination. The chance of discovering sunken treasure worth a fortune is one reason that shipwrecks have continued to fascinate people for centuries.

The 1715 Fleet

During the year 1715, treasure had been piling up. Warehouses at ports in the New World were filling with treasure that was to be shipped to Madrid. No treasure ships had sailed to Spain for two years for fear of attack by pirates. The Spanish decided they could wait no longer. They loaded a fleet of 11 ships with treasure.

The Spanish treasure wasn't only gold and silver. It also included goods that could not be found in Europe, such as cocoa, vanilla, tobacco, and tortoise shell. Some of the treasure was a wedding gift from the Spanish King to his bride.

The fleet set sail from Havana, Cuba on July 27—after the hurricane season had started. The ships sailed up the coast of Florida to catch the trade winds, which would help carry them across the Atlantic Ocean. After only four days at sea, the fleet ran into a hurricane. The ships were driven onto the reefs on the Florida coast, near what today is Cape Canaveral. Ten ships sank. Only one survived. More than a thousand people drowned. The treasure sank to the bottom of the sea.

In Chapter 4, we'll see how these sunken ships inspired one man to become a pirate.

When the Sea Meets the Shore

Strong winds can be terrifying. Yet ships on the open sea usually survive storms, even hurricanes. Ships have been carefully designed to use the wind and to withstand storms. A ship may lose its mast and its hull may be damaged, but the ship usually stays afloat. Actually, ships are in the most danger when they are in sight of land.

Most wrecks happen when wind and waves drive ships onto rocks

reef: A narrow ridge of rocks, sand or coral at, or just below, the surface of the water.

and reefs. With the ship pinned to the rocks, the sea can do its greatest damage. The force of the waves smashes the ship against the rocks and wrecks it. The smaller the ship, the less chance it has to survive. People sometimes escape a sinking ship in lifeboats, only to be pounded against a rocky shore.

How Strong Are Waves?

A wave six-feet high and three-feet wide contains about four tons of water. That's about the weight of a small truck. In a severe storm, that wave can have tremendous force. A ship 100-yards long would be hit by the weight of about 200 large moving vans. It's no wonder waves can do so much damage.

Steam Power Versus Wave Power

You might think that once ships were built of iron and powered by steam they would survive storms. That wasn't always the case.

The *Royal Charter* was a big steamship made of iron. It weighed 2,719 tons. In 1859 it was sailing from Melbourne, Australia, to Liverpool, England. Many of the passengers were returning to London after striking it rich in Australia's goldfields. Their journey was nearly over. Maybe they were thinking that luck was with them because the nearly 12,000 mile trip had gone smoothly. Their luck was about to change.

A steamship

The *Royal Charter* got caught in a fierce storm on the Irish Sea that drove the ship onto the island of Anglesey. A huge wave crashed onto the ship and broke its iron hull in two. The ship was smashed to pieces.

One piece of iron from the ship was found with a gold bar and gold coins stuck in it. The waves were so strong, the gold was pushed into iron as if iron were as soft as cheese. Of the 388 passengers on board, only 20 survived. Most of the passengers were battered to death on the rocks by the waves.

Bound for India

Modern sailors have accurate sea charts that tell them where to find every rock and reef. When parts of the world were still unexplored, maps and sea charts were not always so accurate. Incorrect charts made sailing more dangerous.

In 1755, a fleet of five British ships set sail for India. Aboard one ship was the British statesman Robert Clive, known as Clive of India. (Clive was famous for keeping control of India for Britain.) Mr. Clive's baggage, which included three chests of gold and silver, was stowed on a different ship—the *Dodington*.

As the fleet sailed around the Cape of Good Hope at the southern tip of Africa, the weather grew stormy. The *Dodington* lost sight of the other ships.

Chaos Island

The captain of the *Dodington* studied his charts and calculated the ship's course as best he could. He tried using his sextant, to measure the ship's position, but it was useless in the terrible weather.

A sextant uses the sun, moon, or stars to find position.

So the captain headed northeast to make sure that they sailed further from the dangerous, rocky coast. Unfortunately, his charts were incorrect.

The course the captain set aimed the ship straight at Chaos Island. The ship ran into the

24

island and was completely smashed in less than 20 minutes. More than 200 men, including the captain, lost their lives. Clive of India never saw his chests of valuables again.

The *Dodington* was not the first ship to be wrecked on Chaos Island. Chaos Island was shown in the wrong place on many 18th-century sea charts. British Navy charts at that time named it "Confused Island" because mapmakers couldn't agree on its location.

Mapmakers finally determined the island's true location and placed it correctly on charts. Now, the island was no longer such a threat to safety at sea. That's when its name was changed to Bird Island.

Danger in Still Waters

Even when the wind and water are still, fog and ice can be dangerous to ships. Windless conditions are perfect for fog formation. Heavy fog can limit visibility and lead to a collision with another ship.

The *Andrea Doria*, was an expensive Italian ocean liner. It was one of the largest, fastest, and most

collision: An accident in which two objects crash into each other.

luxurious ships afloat in its day. In 1956 the *Andrea Doria* was sailing from New York to Europe when it ran into thick fog off the Massachusetts coast near Nantucket Island. The *Stockholm*, a Swedish ship, was in the same thick fog.

The fog was dense. Radar was the only way one ship could tell where the other ship was. Both crews misjudged the other ship's positions on the radar. Suddenly, they saw each other's lights through the fog.

The captain of the *Stockholm* turned his ship to avoid a collision. He turned wrong. The bow of the *Stockholm* had been specially strengthened to break through ice. That super-strong bow ripped a 30-foot gash in the side of the *Andrea Doria* and 51 passengers drowned.

A U.S. Coast Guard vessel wanted to tow the damaged ship to shallow water. There the ocean liner might have been saved. But the *Andrea Doria* was not a U.S. ship. The Coast Guard needed special permission to move it. Although the ship stayed afloat for 11 hours, the *Andrea Doria* sank before the permit arrived.

Icebergs Aren't So Cool

In colder parts of the world, sailors have to keep a sharp lookout for icebergs. Unlike reefs and rocks, icebergs melt and move, and they aren't marked on sea charts.

In 1849 the *Maria* was on the last leg of a voyage from Ireland to Canada. In the cold waters, the ship collided with an iceberg and sank, with the loss of 109 lives. Only three survivors were rescued from one of the ship's lifeboats. On the following day, nine more survivors were found drifting on a chunk of ice.

Perhaps the most famous shipwreck of all is the wreck of the *Titanic*. The *Titanic* was a luxury liner sailing from England to New York in 1912. The ship was on its maiden voyage. Newspapers called it the "unsinkable ship."

The night of the wreck, lookouts on the ship saw the iceberg in the darkness. But the ship was traveling too fast to avoid hitting it. Although the collision was hardly felt by the passengers, the *Titanic* sank in two hours. There were not enough lifeboats on the

An iceberg

"unsinkable ship" for all of the passengers. That night 1,517 people died in the icy waters of the North Atlantic Ocean.

Oily Wreck

Today, sailors have modern navigational equipment. They can communicate with people on the shore and with other ships. Sailors have charts they can rely on and huge, strong ships made of steel. Even so, ships still get wrecked.

A famous accident—and environmental disaster—of our time is the *Exxon Valdez* incident. It was rocks, not ice, that stopped this supertanker.

The *Exxon Valdez* is one of the largest vessels on water—almost a 1,000 feet long. It moves with tremendous force through the water. At its top speed of 16 mph, it takes 3 miles for the tanker to come to a stop.

On March 23, 1989, the *Valdez* set off from Port Valdez in Alaska.

navigational equipment: Tools that find out where a ship is, where it's going, and how far it has gone.

incident: A bad event.

The tanker was bound for Long Beach, California, five and a half days away. It was heading south through Prince William Sound. Then the ship changed course because some small icebergs (growlers) had drifted into the Sound. (Growlers are chunks of ice that make a growling noise when they are knocked against a ship's hull.)

Run Aground

At four minutes past midnight on March 24th, the *Exxon Valdez*, loaded with 10.8 million barrels of oil, ran aground. It hit bottom on Bligh Reef.

The impact ripped through the ship's cargo tanks. Tons of oil spilled into the Sound so quickly that it created waves of oil three feet high. This was the worst oil spill in U.S. history. It killed 500,000 birds, 3,500 otters, and 300 harbor seals. The company that owned the tanker had to pay more than $5 billion to fix the damage.

We don't know how the accident happened. Was the order to change back to the original course given too late? Did the helmsman not follow orders? Was something wrong with the steering system? We'll probably never know.

helmsman: The person who steers the ship.

Imagine . . .

the year is 1545. You are Dick Lacey, a young trumpeter on board King Henry VIII's favorite ship, the Mary Rose.

Dick stood on the deck of the *Mary Rose*, nervously polishing his trumpet on his sleeve. He had never felt so proud in his 13 short years.

There was not a breath of wind in the air. For the past hour, the French fleet had used their guns to pound the anchored English ships with round after round. The French galleys were powered by oars. The English ships depended on the wind. Without wind, the English ships couldn't move.

Then a light breeze blew. A murmur of hope went up in the English fleet as their ships swung toward the French. Whistles blew. Dick heard the sailors chant as they strained to haul up the heavy anchors of the fleet. "Haul! Haul! Haul one and all! Haul!" Dick's hands felt sweaty against the trumpet. He wiped them nervously on his tunic.

One of the officers called out Sir George Carew's order. Sir George was the captain of the *Mary Rose,* the king's favorite ship. The yardmen began to loose the sails.

"How are we supposed to fight with our bellies empty?" grumbled a sailor standing next to Dick.

"I couldn't eat if you paid me," said an archer. "My guts ache with sickness."

In his dreams of glory, Dick had not imagined the king's sailors would act this way.

The sailors moved sluggishly into action. Dick watched as they threw a huge rope net above his head and across the main gundeck of the ship. Dick felt a little safer in this cage of ropes. The strong rope net would stop any

French soldiers from boarding the ship. The soldiers and archers took positions in the tall raised parts—called castles—at both ends of the ship. More than 300 extra fighting men had been added to the *Mary Rose*'s usual crew.

"What does that puffed-up parrot know about sailing a warship?" asked one sailor softly. "I've served in more battles than Carew has."

"I think you should just obey your orders," Dick blurted out.

The sailor was ready to clip Dick on the ear when the ship tilted as the sails filled with wind. Dick moved out of the sailor's reach.

The officer was shouting more orders. The *Mary Rose* moved toward the French fleet, her sails billowing. Dick sighed with relief. At last they could attack the French.

The tilt on the deck got steeper. The *Mary Rose* failed to settle back to an even keel. A shout came from below that the sea was pouring through the gunports. Guns and cannonballs started to roll over to the side. Soldiers stumbled on the sloping decks. The boatswain shouted orders to shorten sails.

Sailors scrambled to obey but were caught in the confusion of soldiers falling and tripping.

Cold green water was lapping onto the deck. Cries of panic spread among the men. The rope nets had them trapped. Men were screaming as they slid down into the water.

Dick began to slide too, but a hand behind him grasped his tunic at the neck. The sailor who had been ready to clip his ear had now saved him.

The tilt of the deck got even steeper. Dick watched frozen with fear as the water rose steadily higher up the deck each second. Men thrashed and struggled in the water below. Dick knew that, like him, most of the men couldn't swim. A body cannoned into him. He felt his tunic slide from the sailor's grip. Dick began to slip down toward the rising water. . . .

Chapter 2
Good Sailors, Bad Sailors

THE *MARY ROSE* turned over and sank in perfect weather, killing most of the 500 men on board. Later boats picked up some men from the rigging, which poked above the waterline.

So, why did the *Mary Rose* sink? It's one of history's mysteries. The French guns had not yet done damage. She had survived other battles and was one of the finest ships of the English fleet. Was it the poor discipline among the crew? Did the crew forget to close the gunports as the ship turned? Did the captain order too tight a turn that tilted the ship too far, flooding the gunports?

No one knows why the *Mary Rose* sank. Historians have sifted through records of previous battles and comments by people of the time. They have developed theories. Most of the theories blame the crew for leaving the gunports open after firing. Some historians say that the crew was careless and undisciplined. There is evidence that Captain Carew had told another captain that the crew was hard to control.

The Top Job at Sea

Ships' captains are responsible for the safety of the ship, its passengers, and its cargo. Captains make many decisions. They must carefully choose a safe course so their ship doesn't run into islands, reefs, lighthouses, or other ships. Captains have to decide how to handle the ship in storms. They have to make sure that the ship is kept in good, seaworthy condition. They must tell the

cargo: The goods carried by a ship.

crew what to do and keep the ship running safely and smoothly. In the past, sea captains were responsible for recruiting sailors to be their crew. They were also responsible for keeping the crew well fed and healthy.

Not all captains do their job well. Sometimes sailors refuse to obey their captain. Sometimes good captains made mistakes. Sometimes skillful sailors and captains do their best, but luck is against them.

Crime and Punishment

Jan Steyns was a skillful sailor and the captain of a Dutch ship called the *Zeewijk*. The *Zeewijk* was carrying supplies across the Indian Ocean to the Dutch colony in Batavia in 1727. (The city of Batavia is known today as Jakarta, the capital of Indonesia.) Also on board ship were three tons of gold and silver.

Captain Steyns worked for a shipping company called the Dutch East India Company. The company had strict regulations for ship captains. Captains were supposed to sail along known routes and stay clear of the coast of the great Southland (now Australia.)

Captain Steyns didn't follow the rules. He

changed course, looking for a better route. He sailed the ship straight into the Houtman Abrolhos reefs of the Southland.

The *Zeewijk* was wrecked. Only 88 of the 208 crew members managed to struggle ashore onto a small island four miles long. Somehow they managed to save the treasure. The ship's longboat was saved, and ten men set off for help. Those men were never seen again.

Captain Steyns tried to fix his mistake. He ordered the survivors to build another ship, using wood from the wrecked ship. It took ten months of exhausting work to build the boat. Finally, the survivors loaded the treasure and set sail.

Fair Punishment?

This time they were lucky. The makeshift ship arrived safely in Batavia. Even though Captain Steyns had survived a terrible ordeal and delivered the treasure, he was charged and found responsible for the shipwreck.

The Dutch East India Company punished him

longboat: An oared boat carried by cargo ships.

exhausting: Very tiring.

harshly. Captain Steyns was tied to a pole and beaten with rods. Then he was forced to labor in chains without wages for 15 years. And that's not all—he also had to pay for the court costs!

Not all captains were treated so harshly. Some captains were very neglectful and got away with it.

Speed Kills

In the 19th century, the only way to get from Europe to Australia was by sailing ship. The journey took about 120 days. Passenger and merchant ships wanted to get there as quickly as possible. Ships couldn't travel faster. They needed to find a shorter route.

The shortest route to Australia from Europe is south across Antarctica and then north up to Australia. This route over land is impossible.

If ships could sail around Antarctica, as close to it as they could get, they could still cut many days off the journey. On the return, ships would follow the

Route followed from the North Atlantic

currents around the other side of Antarctica, past South America. This new route became known as the Great Circle Route.

This shorter route was much more dangerous. Sailing so close to Antarctica, ships had to battle strong winds, ride huge seas, and dodge icebergs. Some captains took their ships too close. They arrived in Australia with torn sails and missing masts. Other ships disappeared without a trace.

"Bully" Forbes

The *Schomberg*, a British clipper ship, was expected to break the record for the fastest voyage from Europe to Australia. It was a fine ship with the best and the biggest of everything. It had velvet carpets and furniture covered in gold satin. One sofa was big enough to seat 30 people.

Captain James "Bully" Forbes was in command of the *Schomberg* on her first voyage. He had gotten his nickname because of his reckless sailing, his bad temper, and his obsession with speed.

Forbes often suspected that his crew might desert him to head for the goldfields.

current: A strong flow of ocean water moving in a specific direction.

39

After one voyage, he accused them of crimes and had them arrested.

Forbes left his crew in jail until he was ready to sail. Another time, he told the authorities there was disease on board. He had the ship quarantined so the crew couldn't leave.

On the *Schomberg*, Forbes was so determined to break the record that he flew signal flags that said "Melbourne in 60 Days." Bad weather ended Forbes's plans. Bully Forbes was so angry that he hadn't beaten the record that he lost interest in the voyage. He was playing cards below deck when the first mate reported that the ship was getting too close to shore.

Forbes finished his card game before he went on deck to order a change of course. By then it was too late. The *Schomberg* ran onto a reef. Forbes was more annoyed at the hassle than worried about danger to his passengers. He went back below deck, figuring that the wind would blow the ship off the reef.

quarantine: Keeping people in a small area to stop the spread of disease.

40

Luckily for the passengers, a steamer came to their rescue. The first mate watched over their transfer to safety. The *Schomberg* was dashed to pieces on the reef. Passengers blamed Captain Forbes for the loss of the *Schomberg*. He was found not guilty—but he was never again asked to command a ship.

Scurvy Dogs

"Bully" Forbes was a bad sailor because he was proud and careless. Some sailors were poor sailors because they were sick.

When sailors were at sea for months, their diet was poor. They lived on long-lasting foods such as salted meat and hardtack. If they were lucky, they might have a few hens on board to provide eggs. They rarely ate fresh fruits and vegetables, so they didn't get enough Vitamin C. Lack of Vitamin C causes scurvy.

Sailors with scurvy got inflamed gums and horrible sores on their skin. Their teeth fell out, and they felt extremely tired. They saw terrible things that weren't really there.

Sailors with scurvy usually died. Sometimes half a ship's crew would be dead or dying from scurvy. Then doctors

hardtack: A hard cracker.

discovered that lack of Vitamin C was the cause. After about 1795, sailors drank lemon juice and lime juice daily to combat scurvy.

A Burning Problem

Fire was one of the greatest threats to wooden ships because there was plenty that would burn. Besides the wood of the ship's hull and decks, there was also the rigging and acres of canvas. Sometimes ships carried barrels of gunpowder and flammable cargo, such as cotton. The ship's lights were oil lamps or candles, and the cooking was over an open fire, so fires could be started easily.

Sailors weren't always as careful as they should have been, either. If a ship did catch fire, the fire was hard to put out because the hand-operated pumps that were used didn't work very well.

Fire Below

press gang: Group of men who force other men into the army or navy.

The ship *Washington* was anchored off Plymouth, England, in 1799. Its cargo holds were fulled with bales of cotton from the United States. One of the crew spotted a press gang coming to force them into the service of the British Navy. Sailors always feared being pressed into service.

The whole crew rushed to hide. The ship's cook dropped his knife as he was hurrying through the hold. He struck a light to find the knife and accidentally set fire to a bale of cotton. The fire quickly spread through the whole cargo. The ship burned for nearly 24 hours. The *Washington* was totally destroyed.

Risky Business

Bad weather can destroy a ship, but bad sailors can be just as deadly. Sailors may make mistakes, but captains have the final responsibility for their ship. If they don't do their job well, then passengers and cargo are at great risk. If you are sailing, choose your ship captain carefully—and hope he has a good crew!

Imagine . . .

you have found the diary of Monsieur Savigny. The year is 1816.

W HAT A TERRIBLE STATE we are in. We have been on this wretched raft for four days. I can hardly believe it, but there are only 15 of us left from the 150 who started on the raft.

These few logs bound together with rope hardly deserve to be called a raft. When we were first cut loose, it was so crowded that our combined weight sank the raft. We were standing on the raft waist-deep in water. Even now, though there are so few of us left, our weight still pushes the raft underwater.

At first, the weather was against us. Two nights of terrible storms drowned many and washed away what food and water we had.

Only wine and a few biscuits remain. By day the hot sun burns our skin.

On the third night, the soldiers drank too much wine. They thought that we were enemies and attacked us with knives and swords. If they lost their weapons, then they attacked us with their bare hands and teeth. They were like madmen. I had to fight for my life against men who were once my friends.

The first light showed the raft was covered with dead bodies. We threw the bodies into the sea. Then we made a terrible decision. The wounded were also thrown overboard, so that our few supplies are not wasted on the dying. That is not the worst of it. . . .

We are a pitiful sight. Our bodies are covered in sores from wounds, from sunburn, and from being constantly covered with seawater. Some of us were so desperate that they threw themselves into the sea among the sharks that constantly circle us.

The remaining soldiers may turn mad again and attack us at any moment. Even one of my friends might imagine I am an enemy and fall on me with his sword.

Then the strangest thing happened. Our miserable raft was suddenly surrounded by a swarm of white butterflies. Though some poor souls tried to grab them and eat them, I took them as a sign of hope. I found the courage to carry on. I managed to convince everybody to throw all their weapons in the sea.

At least now, if we all die on this dreadful raft, it will not be at the hands of each other. We gave up all hope of reaching land and pulled down the sail. We have used it to make a tent so that at least we are protected from the sun. I will lie back and give myself up to the visions of green fields that fill my head. . . .

Chapter 3
Surviving Savage Seas

THE FRIGATE *Medusa* was on its way to the
French colony of Senegal in 1816. There were
24 passengers and 160 crew members on board.
Among the passengers were the new governor of
Senegal and his family. The ship
was sailing down the coast of
Africa in an area known for
uncharted sandbanks.

frigate: A
small warship.

The captain was celebrating the ship's crossing of the Tropic of Cancer. He left the *Medusa* in the hands of one of the passengers. The inexperienced sailor drove the ship straight onto a sandbank.

There were only six lifeboats on board the *Medusa,* not enough to take everyone. The captain jumped out of a porthole to make sure he made it into one of the boats. The officers, the governor, and the governor's family filled the boats. The remaining crew, soldiers, and passengers—149 people altogether—had to make do with a hastily built raft.

The boats were supposed to tow the raft. But, before they had gone far, the sailors in the boats let go of the ropes. The people on the raft were left to fend for themselves.

After 12 days of torture, only 15 survivors were left when a ship found them. The ship had not been sent to look for survivors but to find the 90,000 francs left on board the *Medusa.*

Once the survivors were returned to safety, Henri Savigny and Alexandre Corréard wrote about their experience. Their account shocked the people of France.

Tropic of Cancer: The parallel of latitude that marks the north edge of the tropics.

The captain of the *Medusa* was charged with breaking naval law. The story you just read is based on Henri's account.

Captain's Crime

The idea of the captain being the last to leave a sinking ship is not just a noble gesture. It is naval law. Disobeying it is a serious crime and at the time of the *Medusa,* it was punishable by death. The *Medusa's* captain was discharged from the navy, but he was not sentenced to death. He was sent to prison for five years. Do you think his punishment was fair compared to that of Captain Steyns?

What's for Dinner?

Another gruesome story of castaways comes from the survivors of the *Frances Mary.*

In 1826, Miss Ann Saunders was sailing home to England from America. Also on board was Miss Saunders's fiancé, James Frier. He was paying for his passage on the ship by working as a cook.

During the first couple of weeks of the voyage, they enjoyed pleasant weather. On February 1, they ran into a storm that lasted for two days and badly damaged the ship. They thought the worst was over. Then a huge wave crushed the stern.

Although water filled the ship, the cargo of timber made it almost impossible for the ship to sink. The crew quickly scrambled to rescue the food supplies. Unfortunately, they only managed to salvage some bread and cheese.

A tent was made on the deck for shelter. The captain was forced to reduce rations to one quarter of a hardtack biscuit per day. With no masts or sails, the ship drifted helplessly. Two other ships were sighted, but neither came to help. By February 11, the crew and passengers of the *Frances Mary* had no food left. Sailors soon began to die of starvation.

The Flesh of the Dead

February 12, someone suggested that the only way to survive was to eat the flesh of the dead. The next day, they cut the heart and liver from a dead crewman and ate them. The death count mounted, and James Frier also died. Miss Saunders fought to protect her fiancé's body from becoming food for survivors.

stern: The back part of a ship.

The rest of the crew were too weak to move, but Miss Saunders found strength. She cut up and cleaned the flesh from the dead bodies. Her gruesome work kept them all alive.

On March 7, after drifting for more than a month, the survivors were rescued by a ship. Miss Saunders recovered and later wrote an article called "Narrative of the Shipwreck and Suffering of Miss Ann Saunders."

The abandoned *Frances Mary* drifted at sea for several months. An English ship salvaged it. Then it was towed to Jamaica and made seaworthy again.

Real-life Robinson Crusoe

One of the most famous shipwreck stories, *Robinson Crusoe,* is based on a true story. In 1719, the author, Daniel Defoe, was inspired by the story of a man who *chose* to be marooned on an island.

A Scottish man named Alexander Selkirk was sailing with Captain William Dampier in 1703. Dampier was a good explorer and navigator, but he was a poor captain. He often argued with his men. After a dream that the ship would be wrecked, Selkirk decided he would be better off marooned on an island.

salvage: To remove what can be saved.

maroon: To abandon on a lonely island.

The island he chose is a dot in the Pacific Ocean, about 400 miles from the coast of Chile. Selkirk had been to the island before. He knew it had a good climate and plenty of fresh water and wild goats. He was left ashore with just a few clothes, some blankets, a gun, a hatchet, a knife, a kettle, and a Bible.

For a while Selkirk regretted his decision. Rats gnawed at his feet at night. During the day he was lonely and miserable. As time passed, he began to get used to his life alone. He built two huts. He tamed goats and wild cats to keep him company. He amused himself by singing psalms and dancing with the cats. There was plenty of food—goat meat, wild turnips, fish, and turtle. He flavored the food with pimento, a wild spice.

Dampier passed the island again four years and four months later. He saw smoke from a fire. He found Selkirk on the shore, looking as wild as his goats. Selkirk wasn't sure he wanted to return to civilization. In the end, he did decide to return. In later years he became wealthy, but claimed, "I will never be so happy as when I was not worth a farthing."

Feathered Survivors

Not all shipwreck survivors are human. In 1863 the clipper *Friar Tuck* was returning to England with a cargo of China's best tea. During a severe storm, the ship sheltered in a harbor on Taylor's Island. This is one of the Scilly Isles off the southwest coast of England. The winds were too strong and the ship was driven onto rocks.

The residents of the island managed to salvage and hide most of the tea before the coast guard arrived. As well as the tea, they found some Chinese geese on board. Descendants of these geese still live on the grounds of Tresco Abbey on one of the Scilly Isles.

Strange Tales

Shipwreck survivors have many strange tales to tell. Being a castaway brings out the best in some people and the worst in others. How do you think you would cope if you were cast adrift at sea?

farthing: British coin worth less than a penny.

Imagine . . .

you are Israel Hands, first mate aboard the pirate ship Queen Anne's Revenge in 1718.

THE WIND WAS BLOWING hard, and sharp needles of rain beat against Israel's face. But he'd been at the wheel in worse storms.

Six months ago, the *Queen Anne's Revenge* had a different name and a different captain. Now she was the flagship of the feared pirate Edward Teach, better known as Blackbeard.

Below deck was a cargo of gold, silver, and jewels. The treasure was taken from 18 ships they had captured since they had stolen the *Queen Anne's Revenge* from the French. Soon Teach would be dividing up the treasure. Israel was dreaming of what it would be like to be a rich man.

Suddenly, Israel was being roughly pushed aside by his captain. "I'll take the wheel," shouted Teach. "You can't handle the ship in this storm, you fool."

Israel gave up the wheel. He feared Teach's temper. Once, when he was drinking, Teach had suddenly drawn his pistols and fired under the table. Israel still limped because of the bullet in his knee. Teach had boasted that if he didn't kill one of his men now and then, they'd forget who he was.

The ship lurched suddenly and Israel was thrown to the deck.

"Confound this foul weather," shouted Teach. "We've run aground."

The pirate ran the length of the deck shouting. His blood-red coat flapped and his swords and pistols clanked at his sides. "All hands below. Man the pumps before we sink!"

Israel struggled to his feet and looked over the side. The bow of the ship was firmly buried in a sandbank. Why was Teach acting as if they were about to sink? Most of the pirate crew obeyed their captain and hurried below. Israel stayed where he was.

Blackbeard was a huge man, but he could move quickly. Before Israel could stop him, Teach and six of his henchmen had lowered a longboat and jumped into it.

Israel made a move to follow them. Teach drew his pistol and fired. The bullet hit the mast behind Israel's head. Blackbeard wasn't trying to frighten Israel. He was aiming to kill.

The pirates rowed for all they were worth. They soon reached one of Teach's other ships. Through a telescope, Israel saw the ship set sail. The *Queen Anne's Revenge* was left on the sandbank.

A horrible thought struck Israel. He rushed below. The day before, the holds had been packed with gold and treasure. Now they were empty.

Israel ran back on deck in a fury, his dreams of wealth gone. "I hope you die a horrible death," he screamed across the sea. "I hope it happens soon. . . ."

Chapter 4

Villains at Sea

THE PIRATE EDWARD TEACH got the name Blackbeard because of his thick black beard. He was a big man who dressed in a red coat and carried lots of weapons. He wanted to frighten his victims just by looking at them. To add to his terrifying appearance, he would tie slow fuses in his beard. He lit the fuses whenever he was capturing a ship. When his victims saw the huge pirate with the sparks and smoke coming off him, they usually surrendered without a fight.

Teach's Downfall

Israel Hands got his wish. Blackbeard died a few months later in November 1718. He was killed during a fight with a British naval officer. Legend has it that it took five musket-ball wounds and 20 sword wounds to kill the pirate. The officer claimed a reward of about $165. Israel and the other pirates were eventually captured and found guilty of piracy.

The remains of a ship believed to be the *Queen Anne's Revenge* were found in 1996. The records of the pirates' trial provided important clues that helped to locate the wreck.

Piracy

The 16th and 17th centuries were the golden age of piracy. Shiploads of treasure sailed the seas, and piracy was very tempting. Pirates were very common around the Caribbean Sea, where Spanish treasure ships sailed. The many lonely islands there made good hideouts. There were also many shipwrecked and abandoned sailors, so crews for pirate ships were easily found.

Pirates didn't usually wreck ships on purpose like Blackbeard did. They tried to capture ships, either to use themselves or to sell. Pirates weren't always the best sailors, though. Sometimes they sank their own ships!

Robin Hood of the Seas

Remember reading in Chapter 1 about the fleet of Spanish treasure ships that sank in 1715? A man named Samuel Bellamy heard about the wreck and decided to try to recover the treasure. When he reached the Caribbean, he found that others had beaten him to it. Bellamy liked the idea of making a living by finding treasure. But he didn't like having to wait for a ship to sink. Wouldn't it be easier to capture ships before they sank? He decided to become a pirate.

The Whydah

One of Bellamy's greatest prizes was a three-masted English galley called the *Whydah*, which he captured in 1717. The *Whydah* was a slave ship that had delivered its "cargo" of slaves to Jamaica. It was on its way back to

galley: A large, low ship moved by oars and sails.

England with its cargo holds filled with ivory, sugar, indigo, gold, and silver. Bellamy and his crew chased the *Whydah* for three days before her captain finally surrendered.

No one was killed while capturing the *Whydah*. Bellamy wasn't a murderous villain. In fact, he saw himself as a Robin Hood of the seas. He robbed the rich to give to the poor (himself and his crew). He often urged the captive ship's crew to turn pirate and help him steal from selfish rich people. "They rob the rich under the cover of law," he once said. "We plunder the rich under protection of our own courage."

The Robin Hood of the seas wasn't around for long. After capturing a ship with a cargo of wine, he and his crew drank their loot. They ran into a storm and couldn't handle their ship. Bellamy's ship struck a bank near Cape Cod, and the *Whydah* became Bellamy's watery grave.

Sam Bellamy's career as a pirate lasted just over a year. In that time he captured more than 50 ships.

A Sinking Feeling

John Ward was 50 years old when he became a pirate in 1603. He roamed the Mediterranean capturing merchant ships. On one occasion, he boldly sailed his ship alongside the *Reinera e Soderina*, a Venetian trading ship. He arranged all of his men on deck. Each man had a weapon, so that it looked like he had a huge army. Instead of firing warning shots, they fired straight at the crew and hit two of them. The crew of the *Reinera* were terrified. They didn't put up a fight when the pirates came aboard and took over.

The *Reinera e Soderina* wasn't built to be a warship. Her planks began to rot under the weight of the guns. She began to leak badly. She finally sank in 1609 near the Greek islands. John Ward had moved to another ship by this time, but the crew of 400 drowned.

A pirate's career is usually short, and most die young. John Ward was different. He retired from pirating and went to live in Tunis in Africa. He built a palace made of marble and changed his religion. John Ward died of the plague in his seventies.

Caribbean Catastrophe

One of the pirate headquarters in the Caribbean was the tiny French island of Tortuga, near Haiti. The governor, a man named Ogeron, sent a specially built warship to capture the Dutch island of Curaçao. The ship was called *Ogeron* and the ship's crew were pirates. They didn't get far.

The *Ogeron* was wrecked on rocks near Puerto Rico. One report says the ship "broke into a thousand pieces." The crew traveled on land to Puerto Rico, but they were discovered by local Spaniards. The Spaniards knew they were pirates and calling them, "thievish dogs," the Spaniards killed them.

Bungling Buccaneers

The schooner *Fulwood* was sailing to England from Canada in 1828 with a cargo of wooden chests. The crew knew exactly what was in the chests. They were filled with Spanish coins that were being sent to England as payment for goods.

The ship had barely cleared the Canadian coast when the crew killed the ship's captain and officers and seized the gold. Unfortunately, they hadn't left anyone alive who knew how to navigate. The ship was wrecked before they were out of Canadian waters. The pirates managed to save the chests of gold and bury them on an island. But they were captured and hanged before they could enjoy their treasure.

schooner: Ship with two masts. The mainmast is toward the center and the shorter mast is toward the front.

62

Wreckers

You might think that "finders keepers" applies to shipwrecks. But, even when a ship is wrecked on a foreign shore, its cargo still belongs to its owners.

In the 19th century, shipwrecks were a more common event. Local residents often rescued and took care of survivors. It was also the residents' job to bury the dead. Most of them believed they had a right to whatever they could salvage before officials arrived—regardless of the law.

Wreckers were not just looking for treasure. They were happy to find crates of everyday items such as dishes, clothing, and blankets, which they could use or sell. Everything that could be used was stripped from the wreck. Timber was salvaged for building houses or for firewood. Other items, such as chains and copper, were also claimed.

Some wreckers didn't wait for the sea to provide a shipwreck. They lured ships onto the rocks by covering lighthouse lights and lighting fires on hilltops. If survivors made it to shore, they might be murdered and their personal belongings stolen.

Do Pirates Still Roam the Seas?

The Jolly Roger, one of many pirate flags

Though there are no longer shiploads of thieves flying the Jolly Roger, piracy still exists. In 1997, there were 229 incidents of piracy reported around the world.

Modern acts of piracy take many forms. Thieves in speedboats board ships and ferries to rob passengers. Heavily-armed gangs take over huge tankers.

Nowadays, pirates are looking for modern "treasure," such as electronic goods and oil. Modern pirates, like those from earlier days, will take anything of value. Cargoes as different as sugar and typewriters have been hijacked in recent years. Even today, captured ships are far too valuable to sink. Pirates will rename the vessel and sell it to an unsuspecting buyer.

hijack: To stop and steal from a moving ship.

Heroes or Villains?

Bad weather or bad sailing are not the only reasons that ships sink. What's more, people who sink ships on purpose are not always thought of as villains. The purpose of a warship is to deliberately sink other ships. Yet, in war, each side thinks they are heroes and their enemies are villains.

The first warships had only battering rams, archers, and men with spears to fight with. Later, huge catapults were fitted on board. Catapults were most deadly when a burning ball of Greek Fire was hurled at enemy ships. (Greek fire was a mixture of pitch, oil, charcoal, and sulphur.)

Guns were first mounted onto ships five centuries ago. At first, ships were too unstable to cope with heavy, powerful guns. Most battles were fought at close range with smaller guns. The guns were mounted on the sides of the ships. To shoot at each other, ships had to be sailing side-by-side.

It wasn't until 1854 that the gun turret was used. Then guns could turn to face any direction.

deliberately: On purpose.

catapult: A machine that hurls heavy objects.

turret: A turning structure that holds one or more guns.

Scuttled

You would expect navy commanders to always sink enemy ships. But sometimes they sink their own. At the end of the First World War, Germany surrendered to the Allied Powers. The German forces were disarmed. The German Navy had to sail its ships to a natural deepwater harbor in the Orkney Islands, north of Scotland. The British Navy kept watch over the crew of the 74 German ships.

The German commander, Rear Admiral Reuter, didn't like the idea of handing over his ships to the British. He worried that the surrender agreement was not signed yet.

On June 21, 1919, the entire British fleet went to sea. Reuter made up his mind and quietly spread his order. The entire fleet should be scuttled by opening the sea cocks. A group of children on a school trip watched in amazement as every ship raised the German flag. Then they all sunk slowly.

scuttle: To sink your own ship on purpose.

sea cock: A valve on the ship floor that opens to the sea.

The only sound was of air escaping from below decks and bubbling to the surface. Some of the finest warships of the day sank.

Chapter 5: Introduction

Imagine . . .

you are Francis Rogers, the captain of one of three ships searching for sunken Spanish treasure. The year is 1686.

"COME IN AND SIT down, Francis," William Phips said as he invited Francis Rogers into his cabin. Francis glanced nervously around the cramped cabin. The narrow bed was littered with sea charts for calculating the ship's position.

Francis sat down at the small table, which was already set for dinner. A cabin boy came in and served smoked ham and boiled potatoes. The ale in their mugs rocked gently with the motion of the ship.

Mr. Phips didn't say a word as they ate their food.

"Why has he invited me?" thought Francis. He touched the cold metal object under his coat. "He doesn't know my secret. He can't."

It wasn't until the cabin boy had taken away the dirty plates and lit the candles that Mr. Phips started to talk.

"Francis, I don't have to tell you that it has been my dream to find the *Concepcion* and all of the Spanish silver that she holds."

"Of course not, sir," said Francis.

"It is six years since I first learned about the *Concepcion.*"

"I have heard the story. An old sailor, the only survivor of the wreck, told you that she went down on this reef near a pinnacle of rock."

"I know some of the crew think I am foolish to base my dream on such flimsy evidence."

Francis wiped a spot of gravy from the lace cuff of his shirt. He didn't say anything. He had overheard such comments.

"I have tried my hardest, Francis," went on

Mr. Phips, emptying his mug. "I have dedicated myself to the task of finding the *Concepcion*."

"You have done everything a man could do."

"Yes, for a simple ship's carpenter who could not read and write, I think I have achieved something."

"You have, indeed. You have had the support of two kings of England. This ship, and the other two anchored nearby, have been lent to you by rich and powerful men. They all believe in your dream."

Mr. Phips sighed. "My dream has ended, Francis. This is my second expedition. We have searched this area for three weeks and found nothing. There is no sign of the pinnacle of rock. Not a single silver coin has been found. As their captain, you must tell the men, Francis."

"Tell them what?"

"I want you to tell them that we are going home tomorrow."

"But why?"

"We will never find the *Concepcion*. It was a silly notion. I will die a poor man."

There were tears in the older man's eyes. Francis couldn't keep his secret any longer. A smile broke over his face.

"I would never have thought of you as a cruel man, Francis," said Phips. "Why do you laugh at my misery?"

Francis pulled a heavy rectangular shape from under his coat. He put it on the table and slid it across toward Mr. Phips. The older man's eyes widened in disbelief. There in front of him was a shining bar of silver.

"One of the divers brought it up today," said Francis. "I believe we have found your treasure, Mr. Phips!"

Chapter 5
Sunken Treasure

THE CONCEPCION was a Spanish galleon that left Veracruz in 1641. It was full of silver from Mexican silver mines. The ship was wrecked on a reef called Los Abrojos during a hurricane.

William Phips was once a ship's carpenter who couldn't read. He started searching for the wreck 45 years after the *Concepcion* sank. By that time, both the wreck and the "pinnacle of rock" that marked it, had been covered with coral. This made the *Concepcion* quite difficult to find.

When Phips did find the wreck, divers brought up from it silver and chests full of coins. In all, they found more than three tons of silver, as well as gold and jewels. The treasure would be worth about $2 million today.

Phips knew there was more treasure trapped in the ship's hull, but he couldn't reach it. He tried to devise a way to explode gunpowder underwater, but it didn't work. Phips had to be content with a knighthood and a one-tenth share of the treasure he'd already found. The rest went to the king. The

pinnacle: A tall point.

reef where the *Concepcion* sank became known as the Silver Shoals.

At the Bottom of the Sea

Many thousands of ships have sunk with valuable cargoes. Tons of treasure have ended up at the bottom of the sea. Whole fleets sank in the hurricanes of the Caribbean Sea.

Over the centuries, people have tried to find the sunken treasures. In earlier times, treasure hunters were limited because they didn't have diving equipment. Today, scuba diving equipment is readily available. There are also mini-submarines that can take treasure hunters down several miles.

Treasure Hunters

A diver searching the ocean bed

Finding sunken treasure can become an obsession. Instead of simply looking for adventure, many underwater searchers hope to make huge fortunes. Some historians feel that treasure hunters are not much better than pirates.

The hunters may damage or destroy artifacts.

Much treasure can be bought. You can buy pieces-of-eight and doubloons on the Internet. Some pieces-of-eight sell for between $200 and $800. The price depends on how well the coin was made and if it shows signs of wear.

Pieces-of-Eight and Doubloons

Buried or sunken treasure mentioned in stories and films is often described as pieces-of-eight or Spanish doubloons. What exactly are they?

The unit of Spanish currency in the 16th and 17th centuries was the *reale*. The silver coins transported on the treasure ships were each worth eight reales. So they became known as pieces-of-eight.

Gold coins were measured in *escudos*. One escudo equaled ten reales. The term *doubloon* came from the Spanish word for "double." Each doubloon was worth double the value of the unit of currency below it.

Doubloons were made up of eighty-five percent gold and fifteen percent silver. The precious metals were rolled into bars, then sliced

artifact: An object or tool of historical interest.

73

Pieces-of-Eight

into discs. A mold or die was placed on each disc. Then the die, or mold, was struck with a heavy hammer to impress the image into the metal. The manufacturers were mostly concerned that the weight of the precious metal in the coin was accurate. It didn't matter if the coin was circular or the design was centered. That is why no two doubloons are the same.

Silver Shoals

The bulk of the *Concepcion* treasure was found by an American, Burt D. Webber, Jr., 300 years after William Phips's time. Webber was well prepared and made use of modern technology. Before he started diving, Webber spent years searching Spanish records. He also read the newly discovered journal from Francis Rogers's ship, the *Henry*. He used a device called a magnetometer, which detects metal objects.

> magnetometer: A device that uses magnetic fields to find metal objects.

Just like William Phips, it took Burt Webber two

expeditions to find the wreck. On his first expedition, he found 13 other ships—but no sign of the *Concepcion*. On his second expedition, Webber was luckier. He found the wreck of the *Concepcion* in the first week.

Because of his modern equipment, Webber had no trouble getting to the treasure in the ship's hold. He salvaged thousands of silver coins and a thousand pieces of jewelry in about 11 months. His expeditions cost him $450,000, but he found treasure worth nearly $14 million.

Tobermory Galleon

In 1588, the Spanish sent a large fleet of ships to fight against the English. This fleet is known as the Spanish Armada. The English had fewer ships. But they still managed to soundly defeat the Spanish. The English ships then blocked the English Channel. The Spanish ships were forced to sail around Scotland and Ireland to get back to Spain. Only three Spanish ships were sunk in the battle, but 23 were lost on the voyage home because of terrible storms.

One galleon took shelter in Tobermory Bay, off the Isle of Mull in Scotland. A local Scottish

expedition: A journey for a particular purpose.

clan agreed to help the Spanish sailors fix the ship. Repairs were going well when the ship suddenly exploded. Legend says that a Scottish chieftain's wife blew up the ship because her husband had fallen in love with a Spanish princess on the ship.

One hundred and fifty years later, in 1729, no one could remember the ship's name. But no one forgot the fact that it was a treasure ship. A man named Jacob Rowe became interested in the Tobermory galleon. He invented a "diving engine" so that he could search for sunken treasure. His "diving engine" was a copper tube with leather sleeves. The diver was locked inside and then lowered to the seabed. Jacob Rowe didn't find any treasure.

Another 200 years passed before a team of treasure hunters found the Tobermory wreck again. They excavated it but didn't find any treasure either.

Searching the Library for Treasure

Instead of searching the seabed, these adventurers would have been better off searching the libraries.

Detailed records of the Spanish Armada can be found in Spanish archives. If the treasure hunters had searched the archives, they would have found that the *San Juan de Sicilia*, the Tobermory galleon, carried no treasure. The research would have told them their treasure hunt was a waste of time. It would have saved them a lot of money, too.

Pirate Wreck

Remember the pirate Samuel Bellamy? He ended up at the bottom of the sea with his stolen ship, the *Whydah*. He didn't get to rest in peace, though. Like many sunken treasure ships, the *Whydah* attracted treasure hunters.

The wreck was found buried under several feet of sand in 1984 by Barry Clifford, a professional treasure hunter. Thousands of coins and much gold jewelry were recovered from the wreck.

Some historians believe that the most important finds on the wreck were not the treasure but everyday items. The items tell us something about life as a pirate. Some items found on the *Whydah* were elegant pistols, a leather pouch, a silk stocking, and a teapot.

archive: A group of historical documents.

All That Glitters

Not all treasure is made of gold, silver, and precious stones.

In the 1980s, a Vietnamese fisherman came across the wreck of a Chinese junk. He was fishing near Vung Tau in South Vietnam when he found porcelain bowls buried in lumps of concretion. He carefully chipped away the sand and shells and sold the bowls to an antique dealer. He then went back to search for more.

The Vietnamese government heard about an unusual amount of antique Chinese porcelain being offered for sale. They sent someone to investigate. They found thousands of pieces of china at the wreck site. Most of it was still intact.

Historians believe that the ship was sunk around 1690 while it was transporting the porcelain from China to Europe. The cargo included thousands of blue and white tea bowls, teapots, soup spoons, and small figures. The salvaged china pieces were auctioned in 1992 for over $7 million.

junk: A type of ship used in China.

concretion: Sand and stones pressed together like concrete.

More Recent Wrecks

Not all sunken treasure comes from ships that sank centuries ago. In the past 150 years, plenty of ships have gone to the bottom of the ocean with cargoes of gold and diamonds.

The British ship *Douro* was returning to England in 1882 after a trip to South America. There were 55 passengers, a load of gold sovereigns, many gold bars, and at least $40,000 worth of diamonds on board.

It was a clear night with a full moon when the *Douro* collided with a Spanish ship. Somehow the chief officer didn't see the Spanish ship coming.

A huge hole was ripped in the side of the *Douro* when the ships collided. The collision forced the Spanish ship back. The Spanish ship's engines were still running so the ship crashed into the *Douro* again. Within ten minutes, the *Douro* was sinking stern first. In the end, 36 passengers and crew were lost.

Grabbing Gold

In 1979 Englishman Nigel Pickford became the first person to try to locate the

sovereign: A gold coin of Britain.

Douro and salvage its treasure. He spent years looking for clues in newspapers, logbooks, and shipping registers.

In 1993 he began searching the seabed with sonar equipment, scanners, and submarine cameras. When he found the *Douro*, he sent a camera-guided "grab" down to the seabed and in through the hole in the side of the ship.

The first grab came up with some plates and wine bottles but no gold. The second grab was full of gold. Pickford recovered all of the gold bars and most of the sovereigns, but no diamonds. They are still at the bottom of the ocean somewhere.

Andrea Doria Again

Remember the ocean liner, the *Andrea Doria*, that also sank after a collision? There were rumors that the ship's vaults were full of jewels and money. In 1985 a team of treasure hunters braved the deep water to go down to the ship.

The team found the ship's safe. It was full of money—very soggy paper money that no longer had any value.

sonar: A way to find things underwater by using sound waves.

grab: A device with jaws for gripping objects.

Another wrecked ship rumored to be full of gold was the Dutch liner *Tubantic*. It had been sunk by a  German torpedo during the First World War. The ship's records stated that the *Tubantic* was carrying a cargo of cheeses. Salvagers were convinced, though, that $3 million worth of gold and diamonds was being smuggled inside the cheeses. They spent ten long years searching the *Tubantic* and its cargo. And in the end, all they found was wet cheese!

Finders Keepers

It would be wonderful to find tons of gold and silver and become very rich. This is the dream that has driven treasure hunters for centuries and centuries. They work very hard, risk their lives, and spend lots of money searching for treasure. Should they be able to keep their riches? Or would it be better to keep all of the finds from a shipwreck in a museum so everyone can see them? What would you do if you knew where there was sunken treasure?

Chapter 6: Introduction

Imagine . . .

you are Elias Stadiatis, a Greek sponge diver in the Mediterranean Sea. It is 1900.

ELIAS PUT ON THE STIFF canvas diving suit. He waited while Captain Kondos fitted the heavy copper helmet in place. It was hot and stuffy in the suit. The air that came to him in the narrow tube smelled of oil and rubber. Sometimes the air tube wrapped around pieces of coral and the air supply was cut off. That was very scary, but most of the time Elias liked diving.

His father and his grandfather had both been sponge divers. They didn't have diving suits in their day. They had to hold their breath. The best divers could hold their breath for up to five minutes.

Captain Kondos tapped on the helmet and gave Elias the thumbs up. Elias lowered himself slowly into the water. Once he was in the water he didn't mind the heavy suit or the stale air. He loved being underwater.

Elias had never dived near Antikythera Island before. The water was clear and blue. Elias enjoyed seeing the beautiful coral and striped fish on his way down. He hit bottom with a jolt. Now it was time to work.

Elias looked for sponges. It was hard to imagine that such shapeless, motionless things were actually alive. He picked up three or four sponges and put them in his collection bag. Then he saw something that made him gasp.

There, on the seabed in front of him, was an arm, pale and bloodless. He looked around. He saw the naked body of a woman with her legs missing, and a horse's head. He realized that he was surrounded by body parts. What terrible place had he discovered?

He tried to get away from the awful place, but he couldn't swim in the heavy suit. He yanked the air line three times. Finally, he felt himself being hauled up. He moved up in slow motion toward the surface. It seemed to take forever to get back up to the boat.

Finally, four strong arms pulled him up onto the deck of the boat. Anxious fingers undid the helmet. Elias threw off the helmet.

"Dead people and horses!" he cried.

Captain Kondos and the other divers looked at him confused.

"Go and see for yourself," said Elias. "I'm not going down there ever again."

None of the divers would go down. Captain Kondos had to climb into the diving suit and go down himself. He took the end of a length of rope down with him.

A few minutes later, Elias felt a tug on the rope. He hauled it up, dreading what he might find at the end. The other men helped. Together they pulled the object in and gathered around.

Lying on the deck was a human arm. It was not flesh and bone—it was made from bronze. . . .

Chapter 6
Shipwreck Science

THE SPONGE DIVER HAD found the wreck of an ancient Roman trading ship. Very little of the boat remained, but much of the ship's cargo was still intact. The ship had been full of bronze and marble statues. Because the ship was so old, there are no records about its voyage. Archaeologists estimate that it is from the 1st century—nearly 2,000 years old.

Elias was a real person. He was a poor sponge diver, but his name will always be remembered among divers and historians. He found the Antikythera wreck.

Mystery Gadget

The sponge divers also found a remarkable device. Historians think it is a astronomical calculator that predicts the movement of stars and planets. They were very surprised to find that people so long ago knew how to make such a complex scientific

archaeologist: A scientist who studies objects from ancient times.

instrument. Since no one knows exactly what it is, people call it the "Antikythera mechanism." The statues and mechanism are on display in the National Museum in Athens.

Marine Archaeology

People from the 1st century would be surprised to know that their lost cargo would be found almost 2,000 years later. Centuries ago, it was beyond belief that something could be brought up from the ocean bed.

The wreck found at Antikythera made historians think carefully about shipwrecks. They had found out that old and interesting things were waiting on the bottom of the sea. They began to realize that shipwrecks held all kinds of historical items—clues to the past. When other ancient shipwrecks were found, archaeologists became interested. The study of marine archaeology began.

Underwater Time Capsules

marine archaeology:
The study of sunken
ships and their contents.

One problem with archaeology on land is that objects to study are often found in burial places or garbage dumps. But those places don't usually hold things that people used everyday.

Wreckage lying on the sea floor

One exception is Pompeii. Lava from an erupting volcano caught people going about life. The ancient city of Pompeii is like a time capsule.

The thousands of shipwrecks at the bottom of the sea can also be time capsules. If the ship is well preserved, divers can find cabins and cargoes just as they were when the ship sank. Even if most of the ship has fallen apart, some items will still remain. Historians can get clues about the ship's instruments, passengers, and cargoes at the time the ship was wrecked.

British marine archaeologist Peter Throckmorton said, "It has become the destiny of the ships that did not arrive to tell the story of those that did."

time capsule: A collection of objects left to show life at a certain time to people in the future.

Digging in the Deep

Treasure hunters blast and dredge shipwrecks. Marine archaeologists look more carefully through the wreckage. They know that many historical artifacts lie at the bottom of the sea.

A Bronze Age ship was the first shipwreck to be investigated by scientists. It was found in waters off Cape Gelidonya in Turkey in 1958. Scientists carefully mapped and photographed the shipwreck site. Then they recorded the exact location of every item before it was removed.

History on the Seabed

Marine archaeologists want to learn the whole story of a wrecked ship. They want to know how the ship was built, what its cargo was, how the sailors lived. To archaeologists, a pirate's stocking or a rusted lamp is worth more than any gold coin. Such everyday items share information about the past.

Bronze Age: Period of history (4000 B.C. to 3000 B.C.) marked by the use of bronze.

All sorts of items have survived shipwrecks. On the *Mary Rose*, marine archaeologists found leather shoes, musical instruments, the oldest known ship's compass, and a backgammon set. On the Cape Gelidonya wreck, they found a razor and olive pits.

Which Is the Oldest Wreck?

The oldest known shipwreck is 3,400 years old. This ship sailed when King Tut, the Egyptian boy pharaoh, was alive. The wreck was found by Dr. George Bass near Turkey in 1984.

Dr. Bass has found and carefully investigated many ancient shipwrecks. He has been called an "underwater Indiana Jones." Swords, jewelry, pottery, blue and purple glass, and a golden goblet were found in the 3,400-year-old wreck.

Modern Salvage Techniques

The *Titanic*, the best-known shipwreck of all, could not be investigated until 1986. It is more than two-and-a-half miles beneath the surface. A piloted, submersible vessel called *Alvin* was used to reach the *Titanic*. It took *Alvin* nearly two hours to descend to that depth. Remotely operated vehicles (ROVs) with spotlights were sent out

submersible: Able to go underwater.

ROVs: Machines used for salvage in water too deep for divers.

from *Alvin* to take video films of the ship.

Millions of people around the world watched on television the eerie voyage around the sunken liner. Maybe you have seen some of this film about the *Titanic*.

It is rumored that diamonds worth $5 million went down with the *Titanic*. No doubt salvagers are planning how to find them.

The *Titanic* has been at the bottom of the ocean since 1912. Some people think that shipwrecks like the *Titanic*, where many people died, should be treated as cemeteries and left undisturbed.

Reaching the Air

Sometimes items that have been in seawater for many years can disintegrate when they hit the air. Artifacts raised from the sea have to be given special treatment immediately if they are to survive.

Lead shot from the *Mary Rose* became hot, fizzed, and started to fall apart when it was taken out of the sea. Glass beads from a nearly 3,000-year-old wreck exploded into dust when they were dried out. When wood is removed from the sea, it will shrink,

disintegrate: Fall to pieces.

crack, and warp. Each item removed from a shipwreck must be chemically treated to save it. Different substances need different treatment.

People once believed that wood could only survive for a few years underwater. They thought that after 50 years it would all be eaten by shipworms. Now we know that if the wreck is protected by a layer of sand or mud, wood can last for centuries.

Raised from the Dead

The Swedish warship *Vasa* was launched in 1628. It was a work of art, covered with 700 carvings. As a sailing vessel, it was a complete failure.

On its maiden voyage the *Vasa* stayed afloat for about a mile and then sank. Because it had been poorly designed, it was top heavy.

Nearly 300 years later, in 1961, spectators watched in amazement as the almost complete hull of the *Vasa* was raised from the waters of the Baltic Sea. The remains of the ship were put in an air-conditioned building on land.

The *Vasa* was sprayed with 21,000 gallons of chilled water every minute so that it didn't dry out and warp. The ship was then carefully treated with a chemical wax. To make sure the ship didn't rot on the inside, the chemical had to penetrate right through the wood. The wax was sprayed over the entire hull once every day for 15 years. Only then did those who were preserving the *Vasa* feel confident they could safely let the ship dry out.

Can Shipwrecks Have Worms?

Shipworms or *Teredo* worms are small, wood-boring animals like tiny snails. They eat their way through the wood in ships. Shipworms eat the wood whether the ship is sailing on the ocean or lying at the bottom of the sea. When wooden ships sink, shipworms keep eating until there is nothing left.

Sailors used to coat their ships with a mixture of tar, tallow, and sulphur two or three times a year. The coating protected a ship's wood from shipworms. Another method they used was to cover the ship's hull with a thin layer of copper.

The wooden hull of the *Vasa* survived because of where it sank. Shipworms like to live in warm, salty water. They thrive in the Tropics. The Baltic Sea is very cold and has a low salt content. Shipworms don't live there.

Investigating the Past

Thousands and thousands of ships have sunk over the centuries. Their remains are waiting to be discovered and studied.

Modern technology lets us discover wrecks that we could not previously reach. It also helps preserve what we find so that we, and future generations, will be able to learn more about our history. There is enough historical material to keep marine archaeologists busy for a very long time.

Where to from Here?

You've just read true stories of disasters at sea, famous shipwrecks, and pirates. Here are some ideas for finding out more facts about these things.

The Library

Some books you might enjoy include:
- *The Atlas of Shipwrecks and Treasure*, by Nigel Pickford
- *Shipwreck*, by Richard Platt
- *Sunken Treasure*, by Gail Gibbons
- *Fact or Fiction: Pirates*, by Stewart Ross

TV, Film, and Video

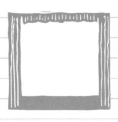

Watch TV listings for *National Geographic* specials featuring shipwrecks and the technology used to explore them. Ask at a video store or your library for films about shipwrecks and pirates.

The Internet

Try your search using key words such as *shipwrecks, Titanic, Andrea Doria, sunken ships,* and *sunken treasure.*

People and Places

Talk to people you know who own a boat or have learned to sail. What can they tell you about the dangers of the sea? Contact the U.S. Coast Guard to ask about the safety rules people must follow when boating.

The Ultimate Fiction Book

Be sure to check out *Deep Water,* the companion volume to *Watery Graves. Deep Water* tells the story of Vincent as he struggles to overcome his fear of the sea and looks for sunken treasure.

Decide for yourself
    where fact stops
        and fiction begins.

Index